$150 MILLION IN ADS

Lessons Learned

JASON BURLIN

Cover by Crislyn Viliran

Contents

$150 Million In Ads: Lessons Learned

IF YOU'RE A marketer who would like advice and recommendations from someone who has managed significant ad spend—then this is the book for you. My goal is to give you the most important lessons I've learned after managing over $150 million in ad spend over the last decade so you can grasp opportunities early in the game and avoid easy mistakes and pitfalls.

I did not start my adult working life as a marketer; I grew up in a small gated community in Israel that was home to many expatriates and immigrants from the United States and other English-speaking countries. However, most people in the community were from California and New York, and the culture they brought with them greatly influenced the culture in that Israeli community. American movies, TV, and general culture greatly influenced me as I grew up and the lure of the American Dream kept me working hard even when things became tough.

At that point in my life, I honestly didn't think I could achieve what I have been able to today. I certainly didn't think I would find a career in marketing and advertising, let alone a successful one. I was street smart growing up, but I frequently struggled with reading and writing and general academics. It made me feel stupid and lowered my motivation to work harder or study because I didn't even believe that I would finish high school at that point in my life.

However, I persevered and learned the best and most important lesson in my life: to practice. No one told me that it didn't matter that I wasn't naturally gifted at reading and writing; with patience, determination, and practice, you can become gifted at anything. Have you ever heard of the idea that you have to put in 10,000 hours to become perfect at something? Whether or not that is true, the general concept is that you will continue to improve with consistent, long-term practice at whatever you set your mind to improve upon. Even Olympic athletes—who may have been born more naturally gifted athletically—still have had to put in thousands of hours to perfect their craft and achieve an elite level.

I believe the same principle applies to marketing; the more hours you spend in the industry learning and experimenting, the better you will become. I recommend always paying attention to any advice or criticism you receive, whether from clients, employees, bosses, or anybody. And as a marketer or business owner, always keep your door open; any big or small company that comes through my doors is an opportunity to learn more, practice more, and develop more client relationships. To this day, I continue to get approached by businesses with great ideas and small budgets. I'm still able to learn new information valuable for my general knowledge from every client that comes through the door.

After struggling but persevering in high school, I finally reached my senior year and decided to move to the United States, where my father and brother were in business. I was working harder than ever because I knew that I would succeed if I put in the work and practice while I may not be immediately perfect at something. By 2007, I started marketing for my brother's moving business. He was an intelligent 20-year-old who was ahead of his time. He recommended I move our marketing services to the internet—specifically to begin to take advantage of Google Maps and their review capabilities. I took the marketing to Google Ads and dominated the ad space in the market because our competition hadn't begun taking advantage of search engine advertising yet. My brother and I joined forces with our partner (who might as well be part of the family and is our partner in other companies to this day), and from there, we opened up more offices across the country in Miami and San Francisco.

This experience with my partners and our success inspired me to learn more about social media, marketing, and paid advertising. It helped me realize that it was the right time to concentrate on online and eCommerce business. Around this time, my wife opened up her eCommerce business and found she could generate sales with organic reach on social media without too much prior computer experience. I stepped in and started working on enhancing our SEO, Social Media Marketing, and promoting the store through Google Ads. My work with my wife's business made me realize how successful you can become when you take full advantage of social media marketing.

However, in the beginning, when we were primarily relying on organic reach, my wife's business began to struggle as

Facebook started pushing paid advertising in the newsfeed to the point that organic reach decreased across the whole platform. We kept throwing money at Facebook content creation, but sometimes we would go a few days in a row without making a single order. We invested in new content and product photoshoots, we pushed our organic content as hard as possible, and we were still struggling.

We quickly found ourselves in $40,000+ debt and had to sell assets to try and stay afloat. I felt utterly helpless and didn't know what I did wrong. Later, I understood that I built my business model and spent my money on organic assets rather than developing our strategies to align mainly with the surge in paid advertising. We began to work towards a new marketing plan, started working with social media influencers, and changed our price model. We began to see the success that I knew was possible.

Once I started to figure out what I was doing with my wife's paid advertising, I decided I needed to do something new myself. I started doing freelance marketing and campaign management. Although I wanted to work for myself, I shelved my pride and started taking small jobs on Upwork or other freelance sites. When I first started managing other people's campaigns, I had significant doubts about whether I was knowledgeable enough to handle other business owners' marketing. I felt very intimidated by technical terms and felt overwhelmed with how behind I was in paid advertising education. It felt like I was back in school, struggling with reading and writing, and unsure I would even graduate. But then I remembered the valuable lesson of perseverance and practice and started reading everything I could get my hands on.

That time in my life when I was trying to catch up to paid

advertising is why I wanted to write this book. There is a ton of overcomplicated information out there from services trying to oversell what you need to learn. With this book, I want to help provide information to you that will break down the overcomplicated technical terms, the myths, the 'tips, and tricks,' and give you more direct information on what to focus on. Marketing has a pervasive culture of following the herd. I can say with certainty that I fell victim to that approach when I first started—it is valuable to learn early that the right or most successful approach is not always the most popular one.

Now, I take all the knowledge I've gained from the experiences I've had, the clients I've worked with, and the mistakes I've made and use it to help lead the 20+ people who work for my agency with the management of campaigns. And now I hope to pass along that knowledge to you!

Paid Advertising Has Changed
For The Better

Back when I first ventured into marketing and paid advertising, everyone thought advertising was a black box. You needed an expert that could manage your campaigns and write scripts for you to automate delivery. Operating the ad platforms as a business owner seemed too complicated and time-consuming. People felt that they needed a middle man to help them utilize the platform for their advertising strategies.

And for most of the business owners who tried, it was too complicated to pick up. It was a challenge to understand how to write the scripts and handle the automation tools. When the platform was built, it required you to babysit your campaigns and be as hands-on as possible. Platforms couldn't even utilize tracking pixels! With the rise of tracking, machine learning, and algorithms, there is a whole set of easy-to-use tools that complete all the things managers had to do manually. As campaign managers and marketers, we continue to witness a dramatic transformation with how automated advertising has become each day. With these changes, we have to learn a new version of the campaign manager's role and determine what we should dictate and what parts we should let the machine learning handle.

As managers now, we can provide goals, help select specific keywords or topics, and somewhat keep track of the campaign. Meanwhile, you let the machine learning fine-tune your targeting to the most efficient traffic based on your goals, clicks, and other metrics tracked by the platform.

Cash Is Your Most Important Resource

I CANNOT EMPHASIZE enough how vital profit and cash flow are to a successful business's heartbeat. If you have huge sales, but you're spending the same amount of money, then you won't be able to build either.

Sometimes a business will show me their background spending information to determine an efficient CPA spend for their marketing budget. CPA, or Cost Per Action, can mean slightly different things depending on how we use it. Generally, it is a pricing model that marketers use to establish how much they are willing to pay for each customer's action to keep their spending goals in check. It is also an available pricing option that platforms use to pay every time a customer completes an action (similar to cost per click, where a user would pay every time someone clicks on their ad). In my experience, I find that companies struggle the most with overestimating the cash flow they have; they believe they have more than they do because they haven't been keeping diligent track of profit and expenses. When the business owner looks at their bank account, they realize they have no cash readily available.

Now keep in mind, I'm not necessarily referring to people who have investors and are primarily focused on growth in the short-term to take their companies public and make the investors' money back. I'm talking about business owners who are self-funded from their own cash or by credit.

For a small or self-funded business, you need to know the exact revenue you need to meet to cover expenses while also making a profit comfortably. And it would be best if you built a business model that incorporates profit in all your decision making. Otherwise, your company will run the risk of tanking in the long term. If you are just starting, then even small changes can make or break your bottom line because you typically have a very tight profit margin. With that, be incredibly diligent about advertising and marketing spend because you can very quickly consume all of your profit trying to concentrate on getting new customers. Without having a detailed knowledge of where your business's bottom line stands on any given day, you can easily back yourself into a corner where a campaign only needs one lousy day to push yourself into the red. The risk of running out of cash and not being able to pay for your ads should be under every business's mind because if you can't pay for your ads, then they will disappear. It is no different from renting an expensive house - if you can no longer continue to afford to pay rent, you will no longer be able to live there and enjoy the lifestyle. If you can no longer afford to pay for your advertisements, then your ads will disappear, and you will stop getting traffic and then stop getting conversions. As advertisers, we are consistently tempted to double up on what works instead of allocating resources to sustainable ends. That creates short term cash but is unsustainable.

You need to understand how to scale your business properly in order to grow your business while achieving a comfortable profit margin. Scaling is the process of slowly working your business up to spend a little more money to increase your overall profits. Ad platforms will continuously try and sell you on new things to try to spend more money without focusing on your earnings, so make sure that you don't get tempted or carried away with your budget on your campaigns without keeping an eye on your bottom line. If you start to scale too quickly, then you will expose yourself to vulnerability with cash flow, where small changes could make or break you. Instead, settle for small incremental growth within your established profit margins to leave yourself a cash buffer—and continue to practice this as your business gets more successful. Even companies that have been stable for a while can be only a couple of bad months away from going bankrupt. Keep your eyes on your CPA: if you begin to notice that your cost per action continually creeps up, then it might be time to adjust your strategy and potentially lower your spending. Keep your operation as slim as possible when scaling to give yourself the ability to increase profit fast.

Don't Expect Profits Every Day and Don't Leave Conversions on the Table

ALL ADVERTISERS WANT their paid advertisements to be successful. Some find their success in trying to scale the campaigns as much as possible, while others feel successful only shooting for steady daily numbers.

However, there is an issue with the latter school of thought. The problem with wanting to keep results steady is that it is based on the assumption that the future will continue to be the same as the present. In reality, you should never expect that the results you are experiencing now to last forever. With the natural ebb and supply and demand flow, it is impossible to expect a good day every day by relying on existing traffic. That's why retail stores measure profits every month as opposed to a daily basis. It wouldn't make sense if they only considered themselves successful if they were profitable every day because the natural ebb and flow for retail are that more people shop on weekends than weekdays, resulting in higher profit days on weekends.

However, with eCommerce, there is a greater chance that

users will be open to shopping on any given day. So when you notice that the platform is estimating an exceptionally efficient day on any given day, you should push your ads hard in order to capture the audience that the algorithm is reading as available.

Let's say that you are currently budgeting for 20-30 sales per day, at a specific goal Cost Per Action. Then one day, the platform tells you that it can get you 50 sales that particular day, still at your goal CPA. Don't miss out on the opportunity by assuming that it will exist tomorrow; you could wake up the next morning, and the estimated CPA is less efficient, and you wouldn't even be able to afford 30 sales. Don't relax when you are getting good results; any day the platform says it can get you more sales at an efficient CPA, you should push hard. Keep in mind that if you have determined a Cost Per Action/Sale that you can afford and that provides you a profit margin that can sustain your business, then do not be afraid to push as hard as possible. Even if you end up spending 100 times more than usual on one day with your overall budget, but you were still within the goal of your CPA, then you will always maintain your cash flow and profit margin. Don't ever leave conversions on the table!

Time is Money

NO MATTER HOW many campaigns you have running or how much money you have invested in paid ads, you only have a certain amount of time to spend per day on your ads. Our most essential resource is time, and if you don't know how to allocate your time correctly, then you're going to be investing it in all the wrong places. I've seen advertisers spend endless hours trying to determine the perfect funnels and strategies only to realize that sometimes campaigns perform better when they are touched less. Think of it as a GPS—GPS is the best example of something that has become entirely automated, whereas before, you'd have to calculate your distance and determine the route. A GPS can auto-calculate for you the fastest route possible and take into account the traffic to calculate the actual ETA. But if you started making up calculations and taking different streets than suggested, then these "external interferences" would negatively impact the GPS's scheduled arrival time. The GPS had to start bringing in the new information and give you new calculations, which slowed you down.

With marketers and campaigns, interfering too much could negatively affect the campaign's predicted results. You can hurt any of your campaigns that use machine learning because the algorithm needs time to learn correctly, and without the time, it can't properly execute its function. This learning time comes into play when making changes to your campaign's bidding or budgeting strategy. That can include changing your CPA or ROAS targets (ROAS or Return on Ad Spend is a metric that measures the revenue you earn for every dollar you spend on advertising), switching your attribution model (a method of attributing which touchpoint in a customer's journey contributed to the conversion), or changing your target spend. It can take up to a few days after you've made the change for the machine to go through learning mode successfully.

Try as hard as you can not to babysit because you could also be missing out on places that could've been improved. For example, you could be completely forgetting to focus on your creative and visual parts of the ads by concentrating only on hacks or tricks to improve campaign performance.

All the romance about a "secret strategy" or a "secret formula" makes one person millions, and no one else knows about it? It isn't true anymore. Previously, there was more manual work to set up campaigns, which created a need for highly skilled and knowledgeable campaign managers to act as the middleman. But now it is so transparent because platforms want you to succeed to continue making more money off of you. With your specific number of hours, you need to be thinking about where your time is most valuable and has the most impact. It is not in things that machine learning has started to take over, like optimization and structure of campaigns—it is going to be on things like your branding, making your customer experience top-notch, and focusing on your product.

The Importance of Branding

MOST PEOPLE ARE generally aware that branding is essential, but people underestimate the actual value of branding. As a whole concept, marketing is the art of selling an idea or vision; this can either be convincing someone to make a purchase or change the way they think about an idea. But branding is what tells the story behind that idea of vision.

You can also understand the art of marketing and branding by comparing it to religion. This part of the book is not to discuss my own beliefs, the concept of religion, or to question any specific faith. But it is interesting to compare the similarities between popular religion and well-executed branding. First and foremost, it almost all comes back to social proof. What is social proof, and how does it appear in marketing? Social proof occurs when people believe that others' choices, actions, or advice are correct simply because of how frequently they occur. Essentially, we tend to gravitate towards the same things that our friends, family, and general community likes, wear, feel, or cares about. There is a similar concept of social conforming in religion; people gather in large community spaces to practice together in a way that reinforces their belief and acceptance of the faith because everyone around them is doing it too. That is why nationwide companies or political opponents will have separate ad campaigns that focus on different values or interests based on where their ads are showing. They anticipate that people will respond best to messages that their friends and overall community are likely to respond to, which is why you won't see the same type of political ads in both New York and Texas.

Another similarity is that it is rarely about the facts. Instead, it is about the story and how it makes you feel. With study and evaluations, many religions have experienced contradictions within the faith or science; despite this, they still have an increasing number of followers. When someone is seeking answers, they are psychologically more likely to accept or settle for explanations more openly for something they desire to believe in. The same concept occurs in marketing when we see a commercial or advertisement for an item that looks exciting, and we purchase because we hope it will work. We don't tend to stop and take a second to look for proof rationally; we just want the solution to our problem or answer to our question.

A business could be selling an item that is not technically any more luxurious than a similar product from any other company, but how they present their product can tell a story that makes you feel like it's luxurious. Take Nespresso, for example; their coffee is great, but it is not so much more exceptional than other coffee brands. However, they want to make you believe it's worth paying the increased price per capsule/per coffee because they have made you think they are associated with wealth and luxury. They fine-tuned their advertising, brought in George Clooney to be in their ads, and restricted selling their products to stores more closely associated with luxury. The brand's perceived luxury allows them to include a "branding fee" in their product price because the consumer perceives it as more premium than other less expensive coffee brands.

This branding didn't happen overnight—branding needs to be established over time, and you can't take any shortcuts. Back to how branding and religion are similar—successful companies and prevalent religions deliver a consistent and repetitive message of their story because repeating the same message makes it more likely to be considered or accepted. And that's just fundamental human psychology. The familiarity—or the more you see or hear something—the more you will feel connected with the message and eventually agree with it. Think of the amount of repetition in the practice of religion—how often do people say and read the same prayers? How many lines of scripture or phrases are repeated over and over?

Nespresso has consistently applied the same concept of how they want to brand their product. Over time, consistent messaging has helped cement their place in luxury coffee brands, and people believe it without any technical proof of its superiority as a coffee. For the business you're starting (or the religion, like our earlier example), the more people you can convince in believing the branding story you are telling, the more likely it will be accepted as accurate. It creates a snowball effect that continues to grow as long as you continue to stay consistent. This also comes back to basic human psychology—we want to wear, eat, buy, or like the same things that people in our community are wearing, eating, buying, or enjoying.

There is also a practical aspect to consistency. If your ads aren't delivering a consistent and cohesive message, then potential customers could be seeing multiple ads of yours without realizing they are from the same business. Not only is this a complete waste of potential audiences, but it could even decrease the value of your brand. Consistency can also help the algorithm learn faster and show your ads to a better and higher quality audience, increasing your potential to make money.

Branding is a long term process and not something that you want to rush. Starting a business with a brand concept in mind and an idea of how you want it to be delivered will save you frustration and make you more money in the long term. If you're going to start an eCommerce business now, then you can hire a company to help you set up an online business from start to finish in a short matter of time. That may be a great resource to get your business off the ground but enables entrepreneurs to overlook foundational steps, such as creating their branding before starting the business.

It All Comes Down To Your Product

As YOU DIVE into the world of paid advertising, it can be easy to forget the most crucial fundamental: you're putting ads in front of people, not in front of a machine. That is a concept that I heavily emphasize with all of my clients, particularly those spending money on ads but seeing poor results.

In this situation, I ask them how many people are purchasing their product. You'd be surprised how many people are spending money on paid advertising and don't know how many people are buying. You may think this is impossible, but it is too easy to get lost in the metrics provided by a platform that does provide real data, just not how many sales you are producing.

Why is it so important to know? Think of it this way: say you own a retail store, and on any given day, you don't know how many purchases were made, how much stock you sold, or how your inventory levels were affected. It would be impossible to run a business that way successfully. It is just as important to have that information in the front of your mind in an eCommerce business, particularly when allocating money for paid advertising. If you're spending money but not seeing conversions and purchases, then it is time to take a look at your product.

I've worked with clients who believe that Facebook and Instagram ads simply don't work because they don't see profits. It is important to remember that major platforms are only for advertising—they can't sell your product or service for you. It is a place that will assist you in showing your ads to relevant people in the hope that they will be interested and click on your ads. Even with a small budget, these platforms are incredibly good at matching your ads with a relevant audience—everything after that is on you! So unless you set up your campaigns completely wrong—which is unlikely—then the problem may lay with your product or offer.

Before you start selling and advertising online, you need to evaluate your product or service first. That is why market research is vital in the early stages; market research will help you determine whether or not your product/service is unique and how other companies have priced it. Market research will also help you determine that if the product/service isn't uncommon, how saturated is the market, and is there still room for you to get a foothold if offers are already out there? If they are, then what are your competitor's proposals, and how does your offer compare? Unless you are fortunate or have a highly unique product, you will always face competition or face it in the near future.

Before launching your ads and spending your money, make sure you thoroughly audit your product/service. All the details need to be complete to ensure a quality customer experience that won't negatively affect your ads' effectiveness. Check your product name, descriptions, prices, web information, creatives, and your landing page. If you are selling a product, then always make sure you run a test order.

Imagine you and your product as a coach and their team; if you have a fantastic coach but a lousy team, then chances are you're not going to have a winning season. If you have an excellent team and an awful coach, your team will probably still do pretty well. That's why I tell all my clients that the product is the first thing to check if your campaign isn't successful. It isn't about your funnel, your strategy, or what hacks you are or are not using: what you are selling is what will make you money at the end of the day. It all comes down to your product.

When you are running paid ads, you have to make every visitor count. If your ad is put in front of someone and they decide to check it out and click on it, then your product still has to be enough to take them to the point of sale. A successful campaign won't just continue to be successful if you swap it out with an inferior product. No matter how creative your ads are or spot-on your targeting is, you can't make money unless people want to spend money on what you are selling them.

Know Your Competition

DURING THE YEARS of working with so many different clients and companies, one thing that has consistently surprised me is the lack of information that companies have on their direct competitors. In my initial meetings with clients, I'd ask them who their competitors were, and sometimes they would believe they don't have any!

One easy way to get a sense of your competitors is to click through your website or start to search keywords related to your business; you should soon begin to see your competitor's ads targeting you. No matter how you find your competitors, you need to be aware of them because you're competing for the same users and audience. Knowing your competition allows you to gain pricing information and evaluate your business model based on what and how your competitors are doing in your market. That will help you to make adjustments to move your business forward and become more competitive.

You also need to understand that not all competitors are made equal—or directly share the same product or service as you. You need to segment your competitors into at least two main groups: direct and indirect competitors. Your direct competitors will be targeting the same audience with a similar product or service to yourself. Your indirect competitors may not have precisely the same product or service as yourself; still, they target a similar audience, or their service/product could meet the same consumer's needs. For example, if you are marketing an online school, other online schools will be your direct competitors. In-person schools may not offer the same business model as you, but they will likely be targeting a similar audience, and someone in your collective audiences could choose to go with the in-person course over your online course. That in-person school would be your indirect competitor.

Competition is still competition, so whether direct or indirect, you need to pay attention and keep track of the amount of competition that exists in your market. It is essential to keep an eye on tangentially related companies to your products and services or your target audience. Those companies could either be a potential opportunity for you to observe or partner with but could become a potential threat within your market. Understanding how saturated your target audience may become will help you decide when and how to re-strategize.

Now that you've found your competitors, how can you utilize the information? You can start by looking into their financials and comparing them. Not everyone realizes how much information you can glean from company financials from a few different sources. Any publicly-traded company must file annual reports and periodic financial statements. You can also often find other business information from the

IRS, a business library, or the Bureau of Labor Statistics. You can even search through news articles to see if there have been any important stories on the business. Not sure what to look for specifically? Always focus on spend and profit first—how does their profit margin compare to yours? How much money do they spend on marketing? Try to find whatever information you can on the ownership, organization, and financials of the business because anything can help you check and see if you should be improving any discrepancies.

You also need to evaluate what your competitors are offering that you aren't. If you're a local plumber and see that commercial plumbing companies that serve your area have online booking and you don't, then you should immediately consider investing in it as well. See what else local and large competitors are doing or plan to do and see if it is worth the investment to stay competitive. That also means you need to pay attention to your competitors' audience - knowing who your competitors are targeting will help you figure out who they are ignoring. Begin to break down your overall target audience into smaller segments and more specific needs. You may find a niche opportunity that your competitors haven't been paying attention to that you can capitalize on. Keeping an eye on successful strategies put out by your competitors can also reduce your trial and error. If a strategy is or isn't working for one of your competitors, then you can reasonably assume that strategy would or wouldn't work for your own company.

If you were in a battle where you had no intelligence on the other army or thought they might not even exist, then you would definitely not be winning that battle. Paid advertising and eCommerce marketing are a battle to get to the top spot to get consumers' attention and money. To win that battle, you need to be fully aware of who you are up against.

Question the Mainstream "Experts"

ONE OF THE most important lessons I learned as I found success in advertising was that just because everyone is saying something doesn't mean it is correct. Over time, so many advertisers fall victim to wanting to be part of the herd to align their strategies to the mainstream thought at that moment. Don't just read the information in a blog and take it as the gospel of truth without searching for other opinions and strategies that are also successful. You can easily fall victim to reading the same popular blogs as so many other marketers and end up aligning with everyone else and promoting the same ideas. Always do your research on who is writing the blogs you are reading; just because someone has presented themselves as an expert doesn't mean that they are one.

The same goes for any data or analytical statistic presented to you; take it with a grain of salt and try to read between the lines to determine whether the data is coming from a legitimate experiment. Ask yourself, what is the cause and effect? Was this adequately tested? Is there a control group? How large or small was the sample size?

Data Can Be Misleading

THE IDEA THAT data can be misleading is an understatement. Data can be manipulated in many ways to make any given metric present a more desirable outcome. Many of the metrics shown to you on various advertising platforms can make your campaign look successful even if you haven't increased your profit. Remember that the platforms will make money off of you no matter how well your campaign is doing for your business, so it is in their best interest to make you feel like your campaigns are successful. With that said, take all the data you see with a grain of salt.

The biggest mistake I've witnessed with businesses is that they use platforms' metrics like ROI (Return on Investment, a metric that measures an investment's efficiency) and Conversion Rate (percentage of visitors that complete your desired action/sale) to track their profits. But you should categorically not rely on the advertising platform numbers to calculate profit because there is no guarantee that it will be accurate and are the epitome of "data can be misleading." First, as I mentioned before, the advertising platform's primary goal is to make money off of you, and they will do that no matter how much profit you are bringing in. Second, any chargebacks, returns, or refunds that happened after the ad-based conversion, will not be included in the platform's metrics and will make your ROI look better than what it is in reality. And as your business grows, there can be costs that you weren't expecting that will decrease your overall profit. Expenses like refunds, disputes, additional overhead costs, chargebacks, merchant fees, and taxes can all contribute to costs you didn't expect. All of those costs will eat into your bottom line and affect your profit but won't necessarily be included in your platform's metrics.

You also have to realize that no metrics are universal across businesses, and you can't deduce a company's profitability based on any one metric. Conversion rate is the best example for this because so many companies get stuck concentrating on making their conversion rate high because they believe that will automatically translate into increased profits.

Say I'm looking at a campaign, and the company tells me that the campaign has an "exceptional" conversion rate of 10%, so, therefore, their business is doing well. Then I look at their product and see that it is a beauty accessory with a product cost of $10. Because of how low the product cost is, a 10% conversion rate does not automatically mean they are making a substantial profit and doing as well as their high conversion rate might suggest. It can be helpful to look at it in the reverse situation as well to understand better. Say there's another company, and their campaign has a "terrible" conversion rate of 1%. At first glance, this seems alarmingly low - but their product costs $100, so they have a high-profit margin with each conversion. So, if both companies had 100 visitors who all made a purchase, they would walk away with the same amount in revenue, even with the two different conversion rates. With two product costs, the companies bring in different amounts of money per conversion to make the same overall profit with varying conversion rates.

COMPANY A	COMPANY B
Conversion Rate = 10%	Conversion Rate = 1%
Product Cost = $10	Product Cost = $100
100 Visitors at 10% CR with Cost of $10 = $100 in Revenue	100 Visitors at 1% CR with Cost of $100 = $100 in Revenue

Conversion rate can be affected by factors outside of strictly making a sale, which is another reason to take it with a grain of salt because it can easily be manipulated. We were running ads for a business, and at first, it operated as expected—when a consumer clicked on the ad, it took them directly to the website. We decided to create ads where you clicked on the ad, it opened another image, and then that second image showed a link to the website. To get to the website, a consumer had to perform two actions; thus, our Conversion Rate dramatically improved because people who accidentally clicked on the initial ad weren't ending up as unintentional visitors to the site. Those accidental visitors can drag down the overall conversion rate, but the website was getting higher quality traffic without them. That higher quality traffic came from that added step since the people who clicked twice were far more likely to be motivated and therefore much more likely to make an actual purchase. It also increased the cost per visitor because we were getting a higher proportion of high-quality visitors.

When looking at the conversion rate, you also need to understand that there are multiple factors at play. The total conversion rate number shown to you includes both new and recurring customers. The returning customer conversion rate will always seem higher because recurring customers are far more likely to directly search for the place on a search engine and revisit the page without clicking on another ad. That will give you two conversions for the price of one click. A large base of recurring customers will cause your overall conversion rate to appear higher, but you can't be sure why your conversion rate is higher without digging into the details. The best way to get an accurate view of your business and conversion rate is to always separate the CR for new customers from the CR for returning customers to plan your strategies accurately. Although analytics programs will show user segmentation, advertising platforms won't always provide returning vs. new customer conversion rates, so you must seek it out.

Conversion rates can also mislead you by not breaking down the conversion rate based on platforms—specifically, search platforms versus discovery platforms. The direct search conversion rate will always be higher because people were already searching for a product or service like the one you provide and are much more motivated to click when they see your ad.

No matter the metric presented to you—or data in general—always keep in mind that you might not be getting the complete picture if you aren't actively digging into it. Looking at your ad campaign and merely checking how much you've spent, and noting your metric's changes isn't enough. You could be receiving positive—but misleading—information from metrics such as impressions and clicks, even if you aren't making sales and progressing the business. Now that the platforms are so user-friendly, it can be way too easy to feel like you're getting enough information without actually understanding if you are being genuinely efficient with your money and making a legitimate profit. Have a firm grasp on your profit goals, your product cost, and your advertising spend and be aware of what metrics the ad platform is basing your results on. With all that information, you can properly and effectively analyze when to re-strategize your ad campaigns.

The Value of the Customer

You know the saying, "the customer is always right"? As new industries emerge and new opportunities arise—particularly in the eCommerce world—business owners and entrepreneurs tend to forget how much the customer and the customer's happiness matter to their success. The potential for cheap customer acquisition during a breakthrough period can be so tempting that businesses neglect their existing customers while paying too much attention to getting new customers.

I can't tell you the number of times I've asked businesses what their repeat customer rate is (the percentage of your customer base that returns to make another purchase), and they don't know. I'll ask them if they survey their customers for satisfaction or what they are doing to improve customer service—and they haven't even thought about it! Many of them don't have answers because they've had an explosive growth period after starting to use paid advertisements and forget to put effort into the process from top to bottom. When a business is in a successful growth period and is acquiring new customers, they need to ensure that they are pushing to keep their existing customers returning to secure profit and cash flow.

To help improve customer experience—and a standard part of the funnel that businesses will forget—you need to ensure that the pre and post-purchase experience is enjoyable for your customers!

Whether you are providing a product or service, it is vital to put effort into the place where you are sending people and ensure that it allows for a positive customer experience. The first time a customer sees your advertisements is your chance at a first impression, and you can improve a customer's perception of your product through an easy to use and well thought out landing page. A practical reason to make sure your landing page and customer experience are excellent is that platforms began implementing a quality ranking to protect user experience quality. So if you haven't considered making sure that your customer experience is of the highest quality, then your ads could be ranked lower and shown less to consumers.

Too many companies forget about this and put their attention into getting a purchase and then moving right onto the next one. But if you forget about maximizing the post-purchase experience, then you aren't maximizing the potential of all the work you've put into getting the purchase in the first place. Marketing strategies typically don't plan out very long in the funnel past the conversion, but that is where a one-time customer can be turned into a recurring customer. A less-than-satisfactory experience means you will most likely be getting a single conversion out of that consumer, and then they will never come back again. Even if you are getting a consistent stream of new customers, it will affect you in the long term because it will continue to cost you more to market your business without the foundation of a customer base.

When you plan out your funnel, make sure you have a concrete plan in place for after a customer makes a purchase. What will you do to retain that customer? Deals or promotions, follow up emails, reaching out for reviews? By putting time and effort into this part of the funnel, you can start to build your returning customer base to match your prospecting customers' level. There is only a finite amount of new people in any given market, but technically you can make infinite money off each person. Leveraging the post-purchase experience will help you continue to make money off of one person (who is already less expensive to market towards). The more money you make off of less expensive customers such as returning, the more cash you have on hand to continue steadily prospecting customers.

I will never stop emphasizing how vital a returning customer base is. I will never cease to be amazed by how many companies don't know the size of their returning customer base or appreciate their potential. Some business owners feel that having a customer be simply satisfied is enough, but truly successful business owners understand that they need to provide a better customer experience than that.

A returning customer base should be seen as a digital asset. An asset makes you money - instead of a liability that can cause you to lose money. All customers are assets, but returning customers are even more so. The real money is with customers who keep coming back to your business.

All in all, the main lesson here is the importance of having happy customers to your bottom line. The best metric to keep track of is Customer Lifetime Value: CLV is the metric that indicates the total revenue a business can expect from a single customer account over a period of time. Why is customer lifetime value significant? Because you can't rely on new people coming to your website every day, you need to ensure your customers' satisfaction, so they return and make more than one purchase (or continue to use your service) without you paying for them to return.

Knowing and understanding the customer lifetime value metric can also help you make better strategic decisions and narrow your focus on advertising. Using CLV can help you determine how much you should be spending on acquiring new customers, based on how much money you will make from them in the long run. If you have a robust returning customer base with a high CLV, you can spend more of your marketing dollars on initial customer acquisition. Even if you spend a significant amount of money on getting a new customer, it will be worth it if they make you a considerable profit in the long term without having to market to the customer again.

You can break down the CLV metric even further to gain even better insights into your market opportunities. By tracking customer lifetime value, you can begin to segment your customers based on the profit and value they bring back to your business. Suppose a particular advertising strategy yields exceptionally high value, high CLV customers. In that case, you can specialize your advertising strategy to those in particular to gain even more profit. Providing a personalized experience—through discounts, providing special offers, or setting up a VIP program—can help retain your high-value customers.

Overall, focusing on the customer lifetime value metric is essential for your company's growth in this industry. The eCommerce market only continues to become more expensive. Customers are more savvy and selective regarding online businesses with a higher customer experience and are more likely to yield a returning customer base. Advertising is so expensive that new brands are willing to break even on their initial order to get a foothold in the market. Established, successful brands with a high CLV won't feel the same strain from increased competition in the market for advertising because they will have a revenue base from returning customers. By concentrating on your customer lifetime value as an essential metric, you will ensure that your focus stays on the customer's experience. You will retain high-value customers better and improve your customer experience and your bottom line overall.

So, how do you calculate customer lifetime value? The equation breaks down to the following:

$$\text{Customer Lifetime Value} = \left(\text{Average Order Value}\right)\left(\text{\# of Purchases}\right)\left(\text{Customer Gross Margin}\right)\left(\frac{1}{\text{Churn Rate}}\right)$$

Now, let's break that down even further:

$$\text{Average Order Value} = \frac{\text{Total Sales Revenue}}{\text{Total Number of Orders}}$$

$$\text{\# of Purchases} = \frac{\text{Total Number of Purchases}}{\text{Total Number of Unique Customers}}$$

$$\text{Customer Gross Margin} = \frac{(\text{Total Revenue} - \text{Cost of Products Sold})}{\text{Total Sales Revenue}}$$

$$\text{Customer Churn Rate} = \frac{(\text{Customers at the Beginning of the Month} - \text{Customers at the End of the Month})}{\text{Customers at the Beginning of the Month}}$$

Now that you know what makes up the number behind your customer lifetime value, you have a list of things you can improve to maximize every customer!

Let's start with ways you can work on improving the average order value, or AOV. If you want your customers to increase the amount they spend on each order, you can try any of the following specialized campaigns to incentivize customers to add more to their cart:

- Set up a customer loyalty program to incentivize customers to increase their cart size to get rewards or points
- Take advantage of product recommendation capabilities—or get them set up—on your eCommerce website. Use these to trigger product recommendations based on what customers add to their cart while shopping on the site, or create an email or newsletter campaign to remind them of product recommendations later.
- Create bundles or packages that customers can buy that cost less than the individual total.
- Offer free shipping to orders that meet a specific minimum amount.
- Next up is working on improving the number or frequency of purchases made by your customers. You can have a high average order value from customers who spend a significant amount of money, but you aren't maximizing your profit if they aren't purchasing very often. If you are looking to accelerate your customer's purchase frequency, then try one of these:
- A customer loyalty program will help AOV and provide an incentive to your customers to be loyal to your brand and continue to purchase to gain more rewards.
- Email campaigns are also an excellent driver behind AOV and purchase frequency. The more personalized you can make the email, the better chance you have of captivating the consumer enough for them to make a purchase.
- Don't forget about investing in retargeting ads! Re-

targeting will help keep your brand in mind whether someone has already made an order or abandoned a cart.

- Your gross margin is the next crucial improvement after working on increasing your orders' value and frequency. If you have customers that are frequently making large orders, but you have a very slim margin of profit, then you won't be maximizing any of your orders.

- Review all your prices, analyze if an increase in prices could be overall beneficial. Invest in price optimization software to mathematically determine what you should price your products to maximize profit.

- Use inventory systems to keep better track of what products sell the best and exactly what your product is costing you. This will also help you reduce any inventory waste.

- Determine where you can reasonably reduce the cost of goods.

Improving your customer churn rate is all about building your customer loyalty and enhancing their shopping experience. As a whole, understanding and focusing on CLV will help you make customer-centric decisions that will boost your brand and bottom line. Breaking down the components will give you better insight into what you may need to invest more time in improving, how much money you should spend on your advertising and acquisitions, and what customers are giving your business the best value.

Becoming a business that values its customers and their experience is always worth the extra effort and planning it takes. A company with customer loyalty and a high customer lifetime value will successfully compete with new businesses or over-saturation in their market. An established, recurring customer base will protect your wallet through market fluctuations, changing product trends, and consistently deliver robust profits.

Build Long Term Digital Assets

WHAT DO I mean when I say digital assets? It's anything that fuels growth and profit—essentially something that will make you money in the long term. That can be either recurring customers or consistent sources of traffic outside of paid advertising that leads to profit. These digital assets protect you from any time you need to turn off your paid ads—you will still have these assets to continue making you money. Always allocate a chunk of advertising dollars to sources that are likely to produce revenue in the long term to balance out when paid advertising might not be working for your business. The overall idea is to diversify your traffic sources to decrease your reliance on any one central platform. Instead, include assets that are likely to provide you a return over many years to come.

So what are some examples? A long term digital asset could be something like a YouTube channel; a growing channel with an ever-increasing subscriber base is a long-term asset because it will continue to provide you with traffic and revenue. Having one viral video is not enough to become a legitimate long-term asset. Still, if you're a makeup artist posting regular makeup tutorials, then you can gain views from old videos and new videos at the same time from new people and subscribers. And YouTube will give you free ongoing traffic to your channel because it is recognized as relevant and featured to the algorithm and will show higher in a search. That free traffic turning into visitors is a reliable digital asset because it will not disappear anytime soon. If you feel your business doesn't work well with YouTube, then find traffic sources through places that feel native. Where do people search or talk about your product or service? What other spaces can be relevant to your company, and how can you leverage them?

Whether it is from a blog or a YouTube video, it doesn't matter if you aren't getting excellent results because all your visitors for that long term digital asset are free. It is called an asset because it can be valued for an actual dollar amount—it is worth money to someone else. Remember that is what makes it different from a liability—it is not something you have to spend money on. Paid ads can quickly turn into liabilities because you do not have control over how much money you need to spend to get the traffic you need.

Another example of a long term digital asset is a high ratio of returning customers that place a few orders a year and consistently return. That is a group of customers that you can count on and will always produce revenue and profitability; many people underestimate how much these customers are worth and the dollar amount that they represent. To use an earlier analogy of renting a house: short-term money makers like paid advertisements are like renting an expensive home. When you're there and making enough money, you can enjoy it, but what happens if your rent increases and you can't afford it any more? It doesn't matter how much money you've paid in rent up until that point; if you can't continue to pay the rent, then you can't continue to live there. A long term digital asset is like investing in real estate; you can rent out the property or eventually sell it. Either way, it can make you money, and the money you invest in it won't be lost or wasted in the long term.

These assets will help you sustainably grow your business in a way that is not dependent on paid advertising campaigns while still driving visitors to your website to convert on a sustainable or extended basis.

I've seen too many advertisers start exceptionally well in paid ads only to have their profits plateau and drop off. They fell victim to using paid ads to fuel their growth without turning that growth into long-term digital assets. Either they fell into a tough spot with cash, their CPA became too high, or their market is too competitive at any given moment—and so they had to turn off their ads. When turned off, their ads are as though they never existed, and their sales drop entirely. You will be tempted to continuously increase your ad spend because these platforms are trying to make money for themselves, but they are also the ones who are driving daily sales and revenue.

I've also seen (and done this personally) too many advertisers fall victim to solely concentrating on advertising on discovery platforms (social media platforms). In that case, it can be incredibly challenging to maintain performance in the long term—my wife and I found this as our initial success from Facebook began to fade. The nature of discovery platforms is that the algorithm is reading what people are personally choosing to look at or read. You can be extremely successful at one point. Suddenly, performance will decrease because people have seen your ads more than once in their newsfeed and are either experiencing creative fatigue from your ads or don't care about your product because it is no longer trending. It will always be challenging to remain profitable when using platforms that can't target people based on searching for an actual product or service, like on search engines. Discovery platform advertising is a constant fight with changing newsfeed and changing trends—it will always be a question of who or what is trending and is currently owning the market. So when you think about how much your company is spending on advertising on various platforms, you should always question if you could spend any portion of that money elsewhere. Is there a better or equal investment that could help you long-term with more stable traffic and sales sources? Treat the growth that you receive from paid advertisements as a natural oil that is scarce, but a long-term asset is a green energy source that will be consistently renewable, and you can get as much of it as possible.

Obviously, this is all easier said than done. The reason why paid advertising is used so widely is that it works. The various platforms invest a tremendous amount of time and manpower into their systems to ensure they give as many resources and tools to advertise as effectively as possible. There is also the obstacle that some niche companies only become successful through the use of paid advertising because there isn't a space for organic or long term asset growth. But even businesses born through the opportunity of paid ads need to find ways not solely to depend on paid reach for the company's survival. It is a massive advantage for a business to understand this early in the game and include it in their financial model to not put all their eggs into one basket due to the lure of short term success. A truly successful business that lasts in the long term will put aside money to other advertising sources or enhance other traffic sources rather than exclusively invest in paid search ads or social media platforms.

If I Could Start All Over Again

Sources of Information

IF I HAD known how important it is to find objective and truthful sources of information, I would've saved myself a lot of time. If time is our greatest resource, we want to make sure we spend it learning from good sources. The difference in where you get your sources of information will separate you from most marketers' herd. Most of the information available out there is not contributed purely to gain knowledge; there is almost always an incentive for everything. Someone might be trying to sell you the product they're writing about or only making money from ads present in their site's content. A best practice is to get information directly from the source; platforms want to increase your knowledge on how to use the platform because the more you use it, the more they will make money. When you are trying to determine how successful a strategy is, look for statistical studies that present hard data. Don't forget about the most essential source of information: your own experience. Every minute spent experimenting is worth twice as much—or more—

than reading. If I had known how much of my knowledge and ability to strategize would come from experimenting, then I would've been much more likely to take lower-paying jobs or "internships" to gain more experience. I can't express enough how much I wish I had shot for more experience in the beginning.

Time Management and Allocation of Resources

As I said earlier in the book—and it is worth repeating—our most essential resource is time. Knowing how to allocate your time to the places where you have the best and most efficient impact is critical to not wasting your time. When I first started running campaigns, I was so afraid to trust others on my team to deliver the highest quality of work because I was scared to lose control. Instead of concentrating my time and effort at the top level, strategic decisions, I wasted my time by regularly doing repetitive and manual tasks that other people could've done. It took a while, but I eventually learned to ask for help when I needed it, trust my team, and understand where my impact would be the best.

With marketing, there will always be manual tasks that are easy to handle but overall time-consuming. There are also creative, challenging, strategic decisions and tasks that need to be addressed, and you need to be able to allocate your time to those roles.

Pick The Right Clients

If I could start all over, I would focus on better picking clients. If you want to be successful as a marketer, you need to determine a level of selectivity for clients and pick clients with good potential, not just any that comes your way. Remember the team and coach analogy from earlier in the book: if a team is doing poorly, the coach is the most likely to go first, even if they aren't the problem.

Not only would I be more selective about my clients, but I would actively try and work with clients from different types of businesses and products. Diversifying your client portfolio is one of the best and fastest ways to gain a lot of knowledge because having diverse experiences is better than having success with a single client.

Learn from Experimenting

I've mentioned several times that a lot of my knowledge has been gained from reading. However, most of my experience has come from experimenting with campaigns and trying new algorithms or machine learning styles. No matter how successful I become, I will always want to gain hands-on experience through experimenting. Without personal experience, you're only learning from other people's experiences.

The more you learn, the more you're able to start to theorize what could work—so put your ideas and theories into testing and experience your marketing theories on your campaigns and dig into the results.

No matter how many people I have working for me, I always leave a specific area of managing the actual campaigns to gain hands-on experience. If you don't use it, you lose it—so always keep practicing your campaign management, creative thinking, and best marketing practices. No matter how you progress in your business, you still need to get in the weeds with it sometimes!

Take the Opportunity When It Comes

If there is one thing to take away from this book—even if you forget everything else—then take every opportunity when it comes along and never leave conversions on the table! Don't allow opportunities to pass by assuming that the same opportunity will exist tomorrow.

Specifically, I would've structured campaigns differently on days when the platform gave me a highly efficient CPA estimate. If I could go back, then I would've dramatically increased my daily budget caps on any day with an efficient CPA estimate to get as many customers as possible. There is no paid advertising crystal ball, and next week you could have several days in a row with an inefficient, too high CPA. Jump on the opportunity when it's available because markets change and trending products stop being trendy.

At the end of the day, focus on using your time and money as efficiently as possible, and you will start to see results. It helps to remember not to listen to the noise: there will always be so many new and different hacks, strategies, or experts. We all would love to believe that someone has the magic answer, but no one does. Every product needs an individualized plan, and common sense and hard data will guide you to choose what will work best for your product.

My mission with this book is to share what I wish somebody had told me before spending a lot of time and resources. I wanted to write what I would've liked to read back then: a straight-forward book that just gives you the truth without trying to overcomplicate things. When I started, I was surrounded by sleazy marketers who were just trying to sell me something. Once I got to the point where I had managed over $150 Million on ad spend, I decided that I wanted to share knowledge and not just receive it; to help other advertisers get started and be the kind of a mentor that I didn't have.

I want you to walk away from this book with the most important lessons that I have worked so hard to learn to save you time to bypass all the trials and errors that I have experienced. Most of all, I want you to walk away knowing that with patience and perseverance, you can grab hold of every opportunity that comes your way and turn it into a successful, profitable business.

Acknowledgments

I WOULD LIKE to thank my spouse: my lifelong partner who has always supported me and helped shape me into the person I am today. To my dear children, my mother, brothers and sisters, close friends and extended family and a special dedication to my father, who is here in spirit with me, and I am sure would have been extremely proud to read my book.

In addition, a special thanks to all the amazing people I worked with, all the amazing brands that allowed me to take part of their journey and allowed me to learn just as much as I contributed and helped them.

About the Author

JASON BURLIN

A SEASONED MARKETER with more than a decade of experience in online paid advertising. Jason was an early adopter of social media paid marketing and has helped hundreds of brands build extremely successful businesses using online paid advertising campaigns. His views on the role of social media marketing are considered unconventional and unique.

He believes strongly in the power of machine learning in online advertising and believes greatly that the way we will advertise in the next decade will be led by computer automation. With a background in psychology, his approach to marketing is based on the perfect balance of human behavior and marketing fundamentals. Jason has been the head of marketing of some of the fastest growing online retailers worldwide.

He believes that actual marketing experience is far greater than learning marketing in theory, and he credits his marketing abilities to the fact that he was able to work with so many different companies in different industries and have access to analyze millions of ads, and an extraordinary amount of data. His key principle for marketing is always product first, strategy second.

https://jasonburlin.com/

www.ingramcontent.com/pod-product-compliance
Lightning Source LLC
Chambersburg PA
CBHW071110220526
45467CB00004B/1780